Praise for

The title of this collection is spot-on: for if ever there was a sorceress of imagery and language, that poet is the magnificent Ashley Dioses. I am overjoy'd to have this new book in my trembling hand.—W. H. Pugmire, author of *Monstrous Aftermath: Stories in the Lovecraftian Tradition*

West Coast Romanticism takes a Gothic turn in these richly imagined verses. Crafted in the tradition of Clark Ashton Smith and George Sterling—yet with a fresh, vibrantly female spirit—voices often missing from the dark fantastic speak out clearly. Witch or valkyrie, selkie or sorceress, each has her own story . . . and the right amanuensis. Ashley Dioses delivers an addictive blend of myth, shadow-dream, and pure emotion.—Ann K. Schwader, author of *Dark Energies*

With incantations both delicate and potent, Dioses' Sorceress teases secrets from the moon and stars, the nightshade and the lily, the creatures of myth and the gilded rogues gallery headed by Lady Bathory. In this exquisite debut, the object of love may be ever-elusive, but the passion it inspires is eternal.—Kyla Lee Ward, author of *The Land of Bad Dreams*

From fae to fantastic, from vampires to Valkyries, from Medusa, moons and maenads, from ghouls and graveyards to selkies and sirens, Ashley Dioses' weird poetry, in sonnet, rondel and other forms, runs the gamut of hellish themes. The inclusion here of tributes to such writers as Poe, Beckford, Le Fanu, Chambers, Lovecraft and Clark Ashton Smith, and even to Sacher-Masoch, Richard Gavin and Donald Sidney-Fryer, does not detract from Dioses' originality of voice. The epic "Atop the Crystal Moon" alone is worth the price of admission. This first collection by a young weird poet proves her a mistress of sorcerous sensuality, weaving a witchery of words that will captivate and enchant.—Leigh Blackmore, author of *Spores from Sharnoth and Other Madnesses*

Nicely spooky stuff, vivid and atmospheric. The poetry of Ashley Dioses makes me wish I were still editing *Weird Tales*. She would have been a natural there.—Darrell Schweitzer, author of *The Shattered Goddess*

Dioses has conjured a collection in the style of C.A. Smith, yet with a fresh perspective that works so well. Her "dark diary" expands as we go. Some notable favorites: "Night Play" where she sees Pegasus with "eyes like molten gold"; you'll be entranced by the magic of her long poem, "Atop the Crystal Moon" and shiver after reading "Bat in the Boiler Room" with lines such as "Beyond the halls invisible in gloom / the bat hung waiting in the boiler room". A remarkable collection, recommended!—Marge Simon, Bram Stoker Award winning author of *Vampires, Zombies & Wanton Souls*

Ashley Dioses' poetry collection sings with a classical style that's accessible, not dated. Each of the four entry sections in this *Diary of a Sorceress* delivers a different version of magical beings, fantastic creatures, desire and blood offerings. The poems unwind like spells, seducing the reader with beautifully formed language. Flowers fill shadowy nights with scents of death and struggling life pressed between pages, withered, yet fragrant. Come *dream a dreamer's dream of longing* with Dioses.—Linda D. Addison, award-winning author of *How to Recognize a Demon Has Become Your Friend*

Here for your delectation, youthful passionate lyric verses of darkness and dread, the greater number of them having a surprisingly upbeat tone as though Love in the key of Gloom means eternal romance, if not High Fetish. Additionally the poet has a delight in Thesauric Discoveries for Goths!—Jessica Amanda Salmonson, author of *Anthony Shriek*

With *Diary of a Sorceress*, Ashley Dioses displays a rare magic with words, assembled into poems that are really spells. Whether she's conjuring a lustful Maenad, the Blood Countess, or lost Carcosa, these enchantments are dark, lush, wondrous, disturbing, and completely hypnotic.—Lisa Morton, multiple Bram Stoker Award-winning author of *The Samhanach and Other Halloween Treats*

Ashley Dioses is one of the brightest talents of the new generation of poets working in the weird verse tradition and a collection of her work is something to be welcomed and treasured.—Peter Atkins, screenwriter of *Hellbound: Hellraiser II* and *Wishmaster*

Ashley Dioses' debut, *Diary of a Sorceress*, is rich with macabre, lyrical imagination. It opens doors to beauty, and labyrinths fraught with radiant blasphemies. Her poetry rests comfortably beside that of *Weird Tales*, Arkham House, Ann K. Schwader, and Richard L. Tierney.—Joseph S. Pulver, Sr., editor of *The Madness of Dr. Caligari*

There is delicate music in *Diary of a Sorceress* by Ashley Dioses. Written in traditional forms, *Diary* is a promising first volume from a new fantasy poet. Filled with uncanny love potions to her beloved, delicious and captivating lines, and rhythmical tributes to Poe, George Sterling, C. A. Smith, and Robert Chambers, *Diary of a Sorceress* shows meter is continuing its fine resurgence in modern weird poetry, and in the work of Ashley Dioses.—Charles Lovecraft, publisher & editor, P'rea Press

Diary of a Sorceress

HIPPOCAMPUS PRESS LIBRARY OF POETRY

R. H. Barlow, *Eyes of the God: The Weird Fiction and Poetry*, ed. S. T. Joshi, Douglas A. Anderson, and David E. Schultz

Park Barnitz, *The Book of Jade: A New Critical Edition*, compiled by David E. Schultz and Michael J. Abolafia

Adam Bolivar, *The Lay of Old Hex: Spectral Ballads & Weird Jack Tales*

Michael Fantina, *Alchemy of Dreams and Other Poems*

Nora May French, *The Outer Gate: The Collected Poems*, ed. Donald Sidney-Fryer and Alan Gullette

Wade German, *Dreams from a Black Nebula*

Alan Gullette, *Intimations of Unreality: Weird Fiction and Poetry*

R. Nemo Hill, *The Strange Music of Erich Zann*

S. T. Joshi and Steven J. Mariconda, ed. *Dreams of Fear: Poetry of Terror and the Supernatural*

H. P. Lovecraft, *The Ancient Track: The Complete Poetical Works*, ed. S. T. Joshi

Samuel Loveman, *Out of the Immortal Night: Selected Works*, ed. S. T. Joshi and David E. Schultz

H. L. Mencken, *Collected Poems*, ed. S. T. Joshi

K. A. Opperman, *The Crimson Tome*

Fred Phillips, *From the Cauldron*

———, *Winds from Sheol*

Anne K. Schwader, *Twisted in Dream: The Collected Weird Poetry*

Clark Ashton Smith, *The Hashish-Eater*, ed. with notes, &c., by Donald Sidney-Fryer

———, *The Last Oblivion: Best Fantastic Poems*, ed. S. T. Joshi and David E. Schultz

———, *The Complete Poetry and Translations*, ed. S. T. Joshi and David E. Schultz

George Sterling, *Complete Poetry*, ed. S. T. Joshi and David E. Schultz

———, *The Thirst of Satan: Poems of Fantasy and Terror*, ed. S. T. Joshi

Donald Sidney-Fryer, *The Atlantis Fragments: The Trilogy of Songs and Sonnets Atlantean*

———, *Odds and Ends*

———, *Ends and Odds*

Donald Wandrei, *Sanctity and Sin: The Collected Poems and Prose Poems*, ed. S. T. Joshi

S. T. Joshi, ed., *Spectral Realms* (2014–)

Diary of a Sorceress

Ashley Dioses

Hippocampus Press

New York

Diary of a Sorceress copyright © 2017 by Hippocampus Press
Works by Ashley Dioses copyright © 2017 by Ashley Dioses
Introduction copyright © 2017 by Donald Sidney-Fryer
"A Page from Jack's Diary" copyright © 2017 by Adam Bolivar.
"My Lady of the Nightshade Flower" copyright © 2017 by K. A.
    Opperman.
"Upon Reading Diary of a Sorceress" copyright © 2017 by Michael Fantina.
"Ashiel's Garden" copyright © 2017 by D. L. Myers.

Cover artwork and interior illustrations copyright © 2017 Steve Santiago

All rights reserved. No part of this work may be reproduced in any form or by any means without the written permission of the publisher.

Published by Hippocampus Press
P.O. Box 641, New York, NY 10156
http://www.hippocampuspress.com

Cover design by Barbara Briggs Silbert.
Hippocampus Press logo designed by Anastasia Damianakos.

First Edition
1 3 5 7 9 8 6 4 2

ISBN 978-1-61498-206-7

Dedicated to Kyle Opperman
for his unfailing dedication, support and edits
and to Dadd for introducing me to poetry and
the worlds of fantasy and the macabre.

Contents

INTRODUCTION

In *Diary of a Sorceress* we possess a remarkable new collection, as well as an exceptional first book, by Ashley Dioses. In this debut gathering of macabre lyrics and longer poems, the Lady Ashiel has assembled almost one hundred offerings under four headings (or "entries"): "Atop the Crystal Moon," "Kiss the Stars," "Star Lighting," and "On a Dreamland's Moon."

These lapidary selections reveal a practiced auctorial hand and a keen and enshadowed imagination. The poet-author has already gained an enviable and hard-earned reputation for herself via the many appearances of her poems in various magazines especially devoted to fantasy and the macabre, whether in prose or in verse. A close poet-friend has aptly dubbed her the Lady Ashiel in the style of the Lady Mariel featured in the narrative "A Night in Malnéant," by Clark Ashton Smith. It makes a worthy appellation and brand-new name.

Ashley's many admirers will surely rejoice at having her well-honed poems (as extant up to now) all gathered in this notable assemblage, proffered under the title *Diary of a Sorceress*. From the first selection to the last, the poet conducts us on a wild and innovative tour of beauty and horror. Many of the shorter pieces in particular showcase her sense of all-pervasive but often fearsome beauty. The "Prelude: My Dark Diary" establishes at once the tone, the voice, that she maintains throughout the entire collection.

The title poem in the first section—dedicated significantly to George Sterling and Clark Ashton Smith, and often drawing upon their oeuvre—captures much of the breadth and height of the Lady Ashiel's vision. It is a vision steeped on the one hand in the poetry and lore of such California Romantics as Bierce, Sterling, Ashton Smith, and Nora May French among others, and equally steeped on the other hand in the poetry and lore of the magazine *Weird Tales*, but especially as preserved in book form by Arkham House under the astute direction of August Derleth, its owner-editor-author.

If the members of this group or school of writers enjoyed relatively little reclaim during their lifetime, they have achieved posthumously a solid fame and reputation. And if they did not establish a particular school while alive, they certainly have done so half a century or more following their individual deaths. Today there is hardly a poet working in the tradition of fantasy and the macabre who does not claim an inheritance of one kind or another from one or more of these elder poets, whose work appears to have assumed the status of Holy Writ, all proportions guarded. We cite at random such representative contemporary figures as Richard L. Tierney, Ann K. Schwader, and Wade German, among many other names.

Into the notable company of these past and present poets, let us cordially welcome Ashley Dioses with her *Diary of a Sorceress*.

—DONALD SIDNEY-FRYER

Auburn, California,
9 October 2016

Diary of a Sorceress

PRELUDE: MY DARK DIARY

In my dark diary I oft speak of things unknown.
The daemons in my mind have now forever tainted
The sirens, pixies, and the vampires there alone.
In my scelestic head, their dooms are ever painted.

My meditations soothe my thoughts yet oft have brought
Grim scenes of death and horrid shadows and red fields,
Where chanting cats of black and butterflies have fought.
Cruel Mother Nature brings dark scenes and never yields.

The many passing centuries have made me weary,
And my still-beating heart has grown so hard, so cold.
From his high castle 'that has grown too damp and dreary,'
A Sorcerer begins to speak with words so bold.

He speaks of love and wishes that there was an 'us,'
But it has been so long since solitude was broken
That I am torn. My heart and head are making fuss,
Yet his sworn vow of love is offered as his token.

Enough of love—this subject hurts my weary head!
My mind has always had some imperfections, though. . . .
Illusions either render one insane or dead,
And yet created fears allow the mind to grow.

Who knows what happens once the subtle snap occurs
In lurking darkness? Thoughts of surgeries precise,
A taste for human flesh, dark spells. . . . My vision blurs
As my mind fills with ghastly visions and advice.

Entry One:
Atop the Crystal Moon

DIARY OF A SORCERESS

Entry One

A tower of new stone stands leering
Down on the shadowed town.
They soon will know of my renown,
And bow before me . . . fearing.

Yet there's another looming tower
Anear where I will stay;
A Sorcerer, I heard them say,
Abides there with some power. . . .

Letters to a Sorcerer

Such an anathema as you
Led me to clearly see
How so delusional your plea;
Notes writ in red to woo.

A heart as warm as sun-kissed earth
Does not pulse in my chest.
The love you seek is a lost quest
If in me you sought mirth.

A SORCEROUS TOME

For K. A. O.

In my one mirror, I am not all I can see.
With blackest goeties ingrained in every vein,
I often scry upon its polished glass and gain
A glimpse of my dark Sorcerer, with book on knee.

He often is engrossed in his old Crimson Tome—
A tome of sorceries—of strange unknowns and lore—
Of mystic incantations, poems, spells, and more.
My wonder grows each time I see it in his home.

THE GLASS VIAL

My mortar and my pestle of green jade
Have grown so black from Witch's Salt and ash.
My glass retort is smoking fumes to aid
In dark concoctions for my potion stash.

My calcinator stands in need of heat
Derived from coals and shards of amber gum,
And my alembic brews black drops to greet
My foeman's lips, which turn from pink to plum. . . .

Liquids of crimson, liquids poison-green
Gleam in the ampoules in my skull-marked case.
A curse in each—none quarrel with this Queen.
I fill tall orders, leaving not a trace.

WITCH LORD OF THE HUNT

In the great briar, the twisting brambles of twilight
Were decked with scarlet drops from thorn-pricked skin of youth.
They had to find the snow-white stag and then recite
A pledge of honor to the Witch Lord and His truth.

His mask was the eburnean skull of a stag,
With antlers reaching high toward the star-filled sky.
This form He did not show, for He'd make hunters brag;
He favored humble hunters, they allured his eye.

His eyes of smaragdine were blazing gems of will.
He was the Master of the Hunt, His will was law.
His furs were draped around Him, made from every kill.
His spear was stained with scarlet drops from flank and jaw.

The Witch Lord of the Hunt must grant a blessing for
A novice hunter to pass safely through His land.
No prey beneath His shelter, be it stag or boar,
Can fall without it, lest the hunter then be banned.

The Witch Lord takes great pleasure in just watching them
Investigate His woodlands, ever in the search
For Him in stag form, till at midnight they condemn
Themselves to sleep. He can depart then from His perch.

He smiles in thought and leaves them in their dream-filled sleep.
He wanders aimlessly throughout his woods till dawn,
For the arousing hunters would proceed in deep
Into His luscious forests, for His Hunt goes on.

"He was the Master of the Hunt, His will was law."

LABYRINTHINE KING

For David Bowie

In lands beyond, an opal moon illuminates
The jeweled goblin throne, where sits the King of Fae.
His eyes of sapphire and of emerald gems create
Enchantments that allure, bewitch, and lead away
Those kindred mortals of wild heart and longing soul.
His love will radiate without a living heart
Beat, for the King of Goblins evermore will stroll
Throughout his labyrinth, no longer to depart.

MIDNIGHT STRIDES

The unicorn and Pegasus are pleasing creatures
And no pure beauty can resist their handsome features.
Always the two of them would nightly soar and glide
With perfect elegance within their midnight strides.
The moon and stars are the sole boundary to stay
Their proud, majestic, sempiternal midnight play.

NIGHT PLAY

So innocent and timeless, wild and rare,
O Pegasus, a wonder to behold!
I saw him once, out dancing in the cold
Beneath the stars, and soaring through the air.
He caught my eyes and stopped to match my stare.
His gallant eyes had glowed like molten gold
When lightning struck, yet still I stood, so bold.
He tempted me to then approach, to dare. . . .

He sprang into the air to soar and glide
Amid the boundless kingdoms of the sky,
And galloped through the graying clouds with pride.
He proudly pranced, displaying for my eyes
His majesty as master of the night—
Yet ere the dawn, he left my tearful sight.

Diary of a Sorceress

MOON ENCHANTRESS

In citadels beneath the sunset's taint,
The moon enchantress shines her light afar.
Beneath the dead and paling stars so faint,
Flames jet from out her moonstone eyes. They are
A white witch-fire that casts a spell around
The lands and seas and hearts of men and Mer.
She is the moon and her enchantment bound
Eternally the sun and stars to her.

ATOP THE CRYSTAL MOON

To George Sterling and Clark Ashton Smith

I long to be atop the Crystal Moon,
Where dreams of marble wharves and silver dunes
Entice my way to magical black mountains
Of onyx spires and obsidian runes.
I drink rubescent wines from jeweled fountains,
Listening to the pomegranate lips
That whisper wicked things between deep sips.
Pale amethyst-eyed nymphs all spin and dance
Beneath rich crimson waters of rosehips
And grapes, as satyrs play gold flutes to trance
The wary constellations to come down
From haunted shores Plutonian, to drown
In aphrodisiacs they so adore.
Sweet poisons scent the blooms atop the crowns
Of faeries from the cosmic courts of lore.
Auroral skies light up the irised pearls
Beneath the crystal water's dainty swirls.
The sirens lurk beneath with tempting forms,
And beck with amber eyes and golden curls,
While their enticing songs call distant storms.
Sleek undersides of peridot just show
Above the sparkling sea, as serpents flow
Throughout the opal foam of turquoise waves.
Dragons unfurl their wings to soar and blow
The fire into the very stars, to save
The cosmos from the ever lurking dark;

"...satyrs play gold flutes to trance
The wary constellations to come down..."

Their emerald eyes at night shine with the spark
Of wisdom. They return to jeweled troves
And curl on golden coins beneath their arcs
Of copper colored scales, in secret coves.
Bedecked with dust from all the shining stars,
The unicorns and Pegasus all spar
And dance and play on Saturn's spectral rings,
Then leave for constellations near and far
On golden rose-hued hooves and moonstone wings.

I dream a dreamer's dream of longing for
Entrance into the Palace's closed doors.
The gem, the Empress of the Crystal Moon,
Hides from my dreams; for her, my heart outpours!
Why must she lie ensconced behind cursed rune?
The goblins murmur of old myths from times
Far gone when she, an empress in her prime,
With Bathorian beauty charmed the men
Of dreams with sweetest songs and luring chimes.
Dull bones were strewn throughout her emerald glen.
Her palace gleams like sapphires in the sky,
With phosphorescent fungi trailing high
Around the towers; and the wafting scents
Of belladonna and azaleas sigh
From poison petals, often to torment
A phoenix caught inside their perfumed mist.
She burst above the vapors and then kissed
The silver sands with jets of sparks and ash.

She soared above the fallen stars and missed
A comet streaking by with fiery flash.
The candy caps of rich and creamy red
Did line the path, emitting fumes that led
Me toward the palace, where I neared my queen.
My love, my Goddess, was the queen of dread,
And yet she was a gem of brightest sheen.
The gnomes and red caps snickered as they read
My mind and motioned me to quickly tread
Behind them, as they led me to its gates.
Bewitched by sorceries intoned in dread,
The faeries wove a casting that predates
The ancient empress and her captors' guard.
The doors cracked open and the faeries barred
The way a moment ere they sought the night.
At last! I would approach her as a bard,
And sing her lovely praises of her might!
Incense diffused from golden censers hung
Above on beaded topaz gems and strung
Amidst the palace halls to drug my way.
The path of smoke was absinthe on my tongue,
For trailing mist of smaragdine display
Ensnared more senses than I dare to tell;
The taste of wormwood wrought its truest spell.
The howling stars protested my ascent
Toward the Empress and her sweetest Hell.
For me, the stars of Heaven still lament.
A garden green as Eden slowed my way,

And luscious splendors lured me nigh astray.
The bleeding hearts wrapped pillars round, to lead
My sight toward the richest fruits of day.
Engorged with juices, red raspberries bleed
And trickle down the freshest spearmint leaves.
A vine of berries black and luscious weaves
Around blueberry pots, and pots of grapes.
Apples of green and scarlet hang from eaves
Above the arches, next to fruit that drapes
The indoor-growing trees of many kinds.
The scent of limes and oranges came from rinds
Arranged around the metal candlesticks.
Lemons and mangoes sat in baskets lined
With sugar-coated pears and other picks.
The honeyed peaches gleamed in pots that spilled
With scrumptious plums so nicely plump and chilled.
The sprawling garden tempted my wet lips,
Yet on I trudged through halls of crystal filled
With opalescent floors that sported chips
Of sparkling nacre and of pale moonstone.
I passed through rooms of diamond fountains known
As home to velvet-necked white swans and koi.
The peacocks rare, of iridescent tones,
Their dominance displayed with pomp and joy.
A fluttering of black wings barely caught
My eye, and yet the lurking creature shot
Through the air quicker than I looked at it.
A chill encroached upon me, I was fraught

Diary of a Sorceress

Abruptly with uneasy tremors fit
For cowards only, I did not know why.
An owl as white as snow sang forth a cry,
And it reverberated through my bones.
Its citrine eyes were set on me, to try
And steal my soul with methods of its own.

The luminous arcades began to dim,
And as I entered the next room, the grim
Expressions of distracted, hot centaurs
Upon me looked, as lamias wet of limb
And scaly skin gazed through their hair of tar.
The sirens lurking in the serpent-pools
Appeared to hint with their two jasper jewels
Of some excitement imminent, and held
Their centaur lovers back, for they'd be fools
To spoil my hunt to find where my queen dwelled.
Then beasts of nightmares prowled the next hallway.
The manticores all snarled and looked to slay,
And creatures of such terrible renown,
Like minotaurs and sphinxes that relay
Sly riddles for those wanting their prized crowns,
Awaited my arrival, yet none came
To hinder me, though they were scarcely tame.
They watched with interest keen and sensed my fear.
I was compelled to go on toward my dame,
For to my queen, I knew I would be dear.
A raven's caw rang out through malachite

Pillars, and black wings fluttered off in flight
Ahead as I instinctively just followed.
The halls to crystal garnet turned, and night
Had seemed to seep into the room, for hollowed
And milky white eyes glowed like rotten stars
From pale and sunken faces marked with scars.
In silks of sarcoline, the pale vampires
Enticed upon mauve divans fit for czars.
They offered wines of heliotrope from briars,
And cherries chocolate-dipped and poison-laced.
Their spell of love envenomed was not placed
So tightly round my heart, for their gemmed eyes,
Their soulless, deathly eyes, chilled and laid waste
To any sweet affection I came by.
Their lust I left unsatisfied; their wine
And food did not corrupt these lips of mine,
And yet caresses clawed my back with nails
Of fiends, for succubi came near to dine.
Their smoky orbs allured me, yet their trail
Of sulphurous effluvium repelled
My nerves, yet my unearthly passions swelled
At their seductive touch and languid breath.
I journeyed onward; all my wants, I quelled;
For only my dark queen would be my death.

Carnelian and opal floors led me
Toward a close of porcelain, with seas
Of sculptured figures, frozen men and lads.

Some looked like porcelain, yet their debris
Of broken limbs showed they were marble-clad.
They were great warriors, or bards of song,
Or poets of the written word, or strong
And steadfast lads who just desired a place
In this dream-world of myth and magic, long
Infamous for its wonders outside space.
I knew then that they were not carved from rock.
A sound so softly echoed, yet her walk
I knew from bygone dream-quests had of old.
The Empress of the Crystal Moon oft stalks
Her guests between her marble dreamers' cold
And lifeless sculptures, yet remains unseen.
Her gown of amaranthine, jewels of green,
And blackened fingertips trailed through her statues,
Yet still, I could not even glimpse my queen!
The scent of almonds, honey-sweetened cashews,
Ensnared my senses, and her lithely form
Beckoned to me and made my blood run warm.
My body ached with fathomless desire
For her, my love, my Empress, yet a storm
Erupted in me, drowning all my fire!

A subtle hiss went sneaking through my head
Like an evaporated flame once red,
Yet was it in my dreams or was it real?
My Empress soon appeared with arms widespread.
Though cold her welcome, still I bent to kneel.

"...for hollowed
And milky white eyes glowed like rotten stars
From pale and sunken faces marked with scars."

Her face was drenched in crawling shadows, yet
Her body pulsed in fervor as I met
Her knee with my too long-awaited kiss.
Her silks revealed a form to make me sweat,
And though her skin was marble carved with bliss,
It now was hued like corpses in decay!
A hiss resounded, and to my dismay,
She had emerged from shadows and her face
Was veiled in silk of amaranth and gray,
Her coiling tresses of a serpent race!
Her cachinnation struck like poisoned spears,
And with a blackened nail-tip, all my fears
Were lifted as she raised me by my chin.
She held no pity or clear crystal tears.
Entrapped, I was her thrall and fed her sin.

The veil was cast aside and drifted down.
Her breath was noxious, but I still would drown
In honeyed fumes emitted from behind
Albescent fangs and lips to match her gown.
Her dark enchanted eyes of jet defined
Abysmal hells, for they were mine to bear.
Awakened Gorgon, she was my nightmare
From yawning chasms rent through hidden dunes.
I stood with marble dreamers in her lair,
Forevermore part of the Crystal Moon.

DRAGONSPEAK

Her scales of molten gold
Lit up the stormy skies.
Her teeth of winter's cold
Were quick to silence cries.

Her eyes were precious stones,
The coldest of sapphires.
Hers matched the Reaper's throne
Of bones, pale as vampires.

Her dragonspeak took toll.
Her voice of thunder's kiss
Has singed the very soul,
Seared skin with fire's hot hiss.

Her claws were swords to play
Against their crafted steel.
She is the one to slay;
When will they ever kneel?

She, goddess of the flame,
Harbinger of fierce pain,
Arises to her claim
Of heavens, and the slain.

Scarlet Autumn Aurora

Such fiery oranges and haematic reds
Illuminate her tresses' silky threads.
She is as hot to touch as is her pique
When her night-darkened eyes should turn to seek
Those souls of sorrow clinging to their shell—
Do they not know it only is a cell?
She reawakens as a phoenix should,
As one that strives to leave this realm for good.
So like a scarlet autumn's bright aurora,
She bursts in flame, igniting all the flora.
She shreds and rips out souls with sharpened claws,
And then begins to wash away their flaws.

FIRE SPRITE

The sizzle, crackle, snap of swirling flame
Burst forth like phoenix-fire upon her skin.
She danced to mesmerize and, with a grin,
She vanished in faint vapors as she came.

LORD OF THE DEEP

A vision of pure awe
Has led me far astray,
That even the crow's caw
Could not turn me away.

Eyes of such ocean green,
And skin of bright sea foam,
Whose likes I've never seen,
Arise from water's dome.

Kelpie, Lord of the Deep,
Surfaces from the waves
To meet his chosen sheep—
A mortal made his slave.

Yet does she even know
It's just his human form
She loves? It's all he shows.
That side is not the norm.

O what a fool she is!
And him as well! To think
A mortal could be his
Is on madness' brink!

Yet I am not a mortal.
A lady of the sea,
I can traverse both portals—
Of limits, I am free.

My honeyed siren's song
Has hardly tempted him.
His fortitude is so strong,
And his refusal, grim.

It should be me he loves!
A lady of great Mer!
One of fish over doves!
O how could he choose her?

His heart, then, I must break.
I can as well catch men,
And her life they will take. . . .
So ends the little wren!

SELKIE

Midsummer's moon reflects her silver beams
Upon the ocean's cold, slow-rolling waves.
I have long waited—how my hot heart raves
To burst from out its cage and live my dreams
Of glimpsing her, my sea-maid! Seal, she seems:
She sheds her sleek, dark skin to dance in service
To the immortal Moon, approaching Corvus.
I must obtain her skin—so near it gleams!

The Selkies dance upon Midsummer's eve,
And turn to maidens on the cooling sand.
And yet without their skins, they cannot leave,
And must avow to take its bearer's hand.
My chance is near. O only she will shine
Within my eyes. In moments, she is mine!

FALLEN ATLANTIS

For D. S. F.

It must have been a wonder to behold
The fallen city of Atlantis old.
Huge abalones gleamed in sapphire waves,
With opal glints reflecting off their cold
And glossy surfaces from shallow caves.

The pillars were of pearl, the cracked old floors
Contained red streams of coral; in the doors,
The orichalch, a pallid flame-gold hue,
Bedazzled the aquatic rooms through pores
And fissures in the palace painted blue.

It was now home to hordes of Merish folks,
The selkies and the kelpies, and their croaks
And squabbles over broken homes and food.
The languid sirens teased the men as strokes
From nacre combs groomed tresses gold-imbued.

MEDUSA'S MIRROR

Ophidian locks coiled round her pretty head;
Despairing softly, they hissed in her ears.
Medusa stood, her heart all full of dread,
In front of her cracked mirror, full of tears.
Her green veil fluttered gently from the gusts
Forever flowing through her darksome cave;
She heard more men with spears, designed to thrust,
And to thrust true, to send her to her grave.

The warriors of the gods sought her cursed eyes,
But she would not be weak to gods or men.
With a shrill hiss, she tore her veil's silk ties—
It drifted to the floor of her old den.
She, clad in marble, watched with a blind stare
When the men failed and left her cold, dead lair.

MORNING'S MOON

The waltzing spirits, once so pale and cold,
Awaited new lives as they shed the old.
Created awesomely, they each would soon
Advance on or decline by morning's moon.

LADY DEATH

All-seeing Death, her kiss awaits for me—
I have forever wanted it to come.
Angelic songs escape my lips in plea—
Her graven figure frightens all but some.
Her faint kiss fills me with such chilled caresses—
Her fragrant breath fast carries mine away.
Her body up against mine, soon she presses
From out of me the life I led astray.

ENTRY TWO:
KISS THE STARS

A SEA OF SNOW AND FROST

I gaze into a sea of snow and frost;
The wind invites with icy grace;
And to its freezing claws my soul is lost,
As I accept Death's cold embrace.

THE ABANDONED GARDEN

The dreaded graveyard blossom, the Nightshade
Of deadly beauty, does not claim this land.
The siren's favored Lily has decayed
From plots of earth where once it loved to stand.
Even the dark Chrysanthemums all shy
Away from the abandoned garden's touch—
Only the red, bewitching Roses lie
Upon forgotten graves in Death's cold clutch.
This Halloween the garden comes to life:
The dead all dance and chat away the night.
But come the morning, they return with strife,
And only withered roses haunt the sight.

GRAVEYARD BLOSSOM

The scent of roses sweetens all behind
The graveyard gates, yet graves so far away
Could not send forth a fragrance so refined,
Like phantom rich perfumes, without decay.
Through veils of vapor, ghoul or goblin follows
Through witching graveyards on this eve of Hallows.

Red candied apples sugar-glazed, and gourds
Are broken on the ground in massive messes
From little witch and ghost and devil hordes.
A few in ruffled tuxes and fine dresses
Have grown confused by these corrupt traditions,
Yet they endure them, trapped in their perditions.

Felines all sense the fae this Samhain night;
The rabbits lead past Otherworldly lines;
Prophets predict things with the mystic Sight;
And priests all pray at candle-lighted shrines.
Yet a lone graveyard blossom lies so lost—
A most enchanting bloom, to cull at cost.

The nightshade lingers oh so silently
Around the rusted iron of the gate.
They kill in stealth, but never violently—
Within the heavy night, they lie in wait
For midnight's mistress of dark spells to reap
Their potent properties of deepest sleep.

"...they lie in wait
For midnight's mistress of dark spells to reap
Their potent properties of deepest sleep."

The purple petals purify the darkness
For trespassers who dare to sneak inside.
The nightshade vaguely does admire their calmness,
Yet trick-or-treaters want what they provide.
The bursting berries lure them all astray,
So unaware its taste will soon betray.

UNDER THE CHRYSANTHEMUMS

Under Chrysanthemums and moon's white light,
The streams of dew drip on the gossamer.
Like shining silk a-sway in chill of night,
They show their ardent glamour in Midsummer
By fullest moon, yet under their display,
The shadows claw toward the darksome sky.
As blooms unbothered grow near shadow-play,
The daemon shadows catch not but your eye.

CALLA LILIES

The lilies of that mournful ground
Form twining scales where they are wanly crowned.
They blossom with a ghostly grace,
And deeply drink of Lethe's cold embrace.
Each urn of ivory entombs
An ochre incense-cone of faint perfumes.
They lure lost souls unto their banks,
Who drink of Lethe's kiss and join their ranks.

—After Richard Gavin's *The Benighted Path*

BLACK-VEINED WHITES

Orchids of sensuous and vibrant shades
Oft seem to dazzle under sunlight's fire.
Beneath blue skies they seldom do require
More tempting butterflies in their green glades.
The black-veined whites, though beautiful they seem,
Are often spellbound by the precious nectar:
Despite the lepidopterous dead specters,
The rivals vie for nectar of a dream.

VAPORS

The violet vapors of the morning's misty glen
Engulfed the sweet-grass and each honeysuckle bloom.
They spiraled and entwined around the oaks and then
Awoke the sleeping dryads and the fauns from gloom.

They blinked the dew drops from their brightened eyes and fled
Away or sought to chase each other till the night
Fell and the stars arose and gleamed in shades of red
And gold. At dawn, the mist came, violet in the light.

THE PERFECT ROSE

To Nora May French

The soft and languid rays of dawn,
Of colors red and gold,
Caress the rose to which they're drawn,
A splendor to behold.

The silken petals painted red,
A scarlet like her lips,
Gleam out amid the poppy bed,
And shine till daylight slips.

The perfect rose, still young and pure,
Still timeless like a swan,
Can heed the storm and its strong lure—
It bloomed, and now is gone.

THE DWELLING PLACE

Within my rustic forest home,
Fresh fragrances fill my new tome
Of primal, prehistoric plants
And lyrical sweet healing chants.
The many withered flowers and leaves
Are pressed in pages, kept in sleeves.
The caramel parchment will entice
Book lovers, moths, and starving mice.

THE MOON

Illuminating from the sky above,
She radiates her aeon-lasting love.
The dim subconscious is her prized domain;
She toys with instincts and she deals with pain.
A light that guides through midnight's black abyss,
She comes to aid at Death's untimely kiss.

KISS THE STARS

Liquid black darkness sears with icy flames.
In it I sink, forever falling, yet
Eternally suspended, all the same.
I am the light that guides, yet still I fret.

O loneliness forsake me, for the Sun
Does not adore me as the legends tell!
I am the Moon, She that most beings shun—
For gazes look upon me when in Hell.

Their hatred slowly brews as I show them
That night is everlasting, as is fear.
They cannot fathom that I am their gem;
The light in their deep darkness when I near.

Who lights the heart of me in my dark mess?
Who but the hot and burning stars, whose breath
Of languid warmth gives me the soft caress
Of a pure love that transcends even death!

Celestial lovers of the cold cosmos
Surround me and, though they are still so far,
Like lovely Venus or red Mars' Deimos,
I, in return, the Moon, shall kiss the stars.

CELESTIAL MYSTERIES

Enthroned above our earthly boundaries,
The stars inspire perpetual unease.
Celestial mysteries incite such fear,
As overhead, they ever seem to leer.
Enshrouded with the darkling lore they hold,
They call to us through cryptic dreams untold.

THE HANDS OF CHAOS

Into the cosmos astral beings burn,
Their flames, their weaving flames, fair fatal fae.
In swirling rhythms, fiery bodies turn
Like sparkling marbles; Hands of Chaos play.

ENTRY THREE: STAR LIGHTING

ONE WINTER EVE

One winter eve by softly glowing lights,
When flowers slept and waking were the sprites,
I longed to just reside in the one fire
Aflame for me within a heart's desire.

To an Unknown Mistress

My dreams are ever haunted by her sight, one such as she;
Her hair was heavy burnished gold that shone like the evening sea.
And her jeweled eyes, O those jeweled eyes, would be just as stone cold,
For only azure from the skies untouched by pale clouds' hold
Could be so painted in those crystalline jeweled eyes of hers!
For lovelier eyes could never be found to cause young hearts to stir!
And for her lips, the very roses rose from sleep to kiss
The ruby reds into her snowy flesh, I'm sure of this.
Alas, her lovely visage, it was just a dream of mine,
Yet I know on a higher moon, a crystal moon, she shines.

—After Robert W. Chambers's "The Street of the Four Winds"

A Queen in Hell

To Edgar Allan Poe

Upon a moonlit eve, we strolled along the shores
Of a still lake, all atrament save for the bright,
Rich, hoary moon-glow, which threw wide dark, eldritch doors
Into a hell of reeking hells that stole her light.

My love, my gorgeous love, how could you abandon me?
What haunting daemons lured you to your early grave?
How could you not perceive that you were always free?
Why, why was it not you, my love, that I could save?

The years have passed and sadly I stand so alone
Beside you, by your grave, yet in my heart you dwell.
Your kinsmen knew of your great beauty, and it's known
That we lament so deeply for a queen in Hell.

EVER FAIR

Your hair of onyx, ever fair,
Has gained the scent of sweetest pear.
Your skin of pallid roses slips
To ghoulish green and ice blue hips.
Your lips of softest petals kiss
My lips no more, no more, yet hiss
In whispers like the wind when I
Submerge your body in the lye.

STAR LIGHTING

For K. A. O.

A light in darkness sparked the caverns of my heart
When first I found, in you, the star upon my chart.
A star of brightest white to rival even the moon,
And just the spark to light my star, and not too soon.

LOVER'S WITCH

The Sun's gold gleams beneath her skin,
And gives its warmth with every touch.
Her eyes are gems, the Moon's blue twins,
Which sparkle, barely hinting much.

A promise of sweet Heaven's kiss
Forever lures me to her hold.
Her gaze upon me is pure bliss,
And that was how my soul was sold.

Her love, a spell, is wound around
My soul, like lingering perfumes
That emanate from floral crowns
Of belladonna all abloom.

She is the star and its fierce fire,
The Moon and its deep darkest phase,
The red, red rose of the great briar,
The center garden in the maze.

When those in favor fall from grace,
Her skin sears with Hell's hottest flame.
Her eyes grow dark with new Moon's face,
And lips give way to fangs' quick aim.

I am her lover; she, my witch.
She, my desire, for only I
Can coax the Moon back from the pitch,
And the fine gold from flame's last cry.

Diary of a Sorceress

"A promise of sweet Heaven's kiss
Forever lures me to her hold."

WITCH'S LOVE

Twin moons of palest crystal set
In cerulean eyes; star-fire
Enflames his crown with ruby jets
As red as Hades' grandest pyre.

My lavender and rosehip blend,
Enchanted with my witch's touch,
Was not used as I did intend;
His heart, at once, was in my clutch.

His taste is honey on my lips,
His silver tongue is sweeter still,
His touch is silk on my soft hips,
His love is master of my will.

He is the cosmos and its ice,
The oak and its deep steadfast roots,
The green absinthe and its high price,
The diamond from the ash and soot.

In only me his interest peaks,
For I alone enrapture him.
In me my magic love he seeks,
For I choose love not on a whim.

I am his witch and he, my love.
He, my desire, for only I
Can melt his ice from skies above,
And temper his poisonous high.

ENCHANTRESS

My magic gives new life to things—
Such things as stones that dance to beats,
Petals that fly like feathered wings,
And honey singing just as sweet.

Why does his heart refuse to beat?
I can't enchant it, make it dance,
For my sole presence does not heat
His heart. I feel I've lost my chance. . . .
Perhaps my soul is not a treat.

DARK POET OF MY HEART

For K. A. O.

With pretty eyes of sapphire I do shine,
Yet there are none that I would have be mine.
They play their tunes with strings inside my heart,
And yet my special love-song makes them part.
With every pull they leave my harp distorted;
When feelings are confessed, theirs are aborted.
Can there be none that would steal me away?
Or do all joy in stealing hearts as play?
Perhaps my heart tires of the songs they pick,
For mine is no mere flame upon a wick.
Perhaps a sound that isn't born of songs—
One filled with words of a good heart that longs.
By quill and parchment I have found the start:
A kindred flame, dark poet of my heart.

DARK VALENTINE

For K. A. O.

O Sorcerer, dark love and skald extraordinaire,
Your offer I accept—we'll make the finest pair.
A vibrant moon above us shines with sweetened glee.
Out in the fresh, chill night our presence makes fools flee.
Together we shall drink on this most treasured night,
To celebrate a darker shade of Valentine.
This night is filled with magic in my knowing Sight,
And we shall come together; you, too, shall be mine.

DARK VALENTINE II

For K. A. O.

O love, one winter passed and now we are still here.
The love we share has blossomed, growing through the year.
I've numbered memories you have bestowed on me;
Without you, I'd have drowned amid a loveless sea.
Together we shall drink again while moonlight shines,
To celebrate the darker side of Valentines.
Our hidden fears were only shone to the Nocturnal,
Yet stronger now, I've made way to love eternal.

My Dark Valentine

For K. A. O.

The wine we often drink from our bejeweled goblets
Has grown so sweet, and still, desiring dark, wet droplets
Left from the cold, we drink for its desired warm taste.
Our love, like wine, grows finer with its age, and haste
Can spoil the finest bonds. Together we create
A lasting tie of wondrous love. To you, Soul Mate,
I ask if you would please be my Dark Valentine.
Alas, I cannot bear for you to not be mine.

THE CELEBRATION OF DREAMS

For K. A. O.

This summer night we drink of sweetest nectars
From chalices of silver, under beams
Of pallid moonlight, Luna, our sole specter
This night, the celebration of our dreams.
Of all the visions that my Sight bestowed,
My vision of you cannot be compared.
My love had slowly started to erode,
Until by true love was my heart repaired.
One year has passed and still our love stays strong.
Our interlacing ardors merge, create
A sorcerous bond, whereby we each belong
Unto the other and our life awaits. . . .

THE FIRES OF SUMMER

For K. A. O.

The fires of summer burned into next year,
And lasted through the harshest winter chills.
My heart enflames for only you, my dear.
The stars alight in your sweet eyes, and thrills
Of love ignite my soul at your mere touch.
Tonight we drink again to love, to us,
And to the years still yet to come, and such
Romantic letters scribed by calamus.

RONDEL TO MY LOVE

For K. A. O.

Till the skies fall, on this fine day,
My love, the rarest gift of all,
I give. A flame that will not gray
Till the skies fall.

Upon this scroll, in red I scrawl
All words my heart desires to say.
My love for you is true, my doll.

Till the skies fall, I am the fae;
My soul enflames and yearns to call
On yours. My love will never stray
Till the skies fall.

SKY FALLEN MAIDEN

Asleep inside a dream of faerie lands,
A maid with richest amaranthine lips
And lavish locks of erythraean strips
Began to waken on the ancient sands.
The rising warmth of sunlight's golden strands
Forewarned her of the outcome she had clipped
From out the Book of Fates, her life's set script.
She feared again she was in Fate's grim hands.

The fallen fae attempted falling back
Into a perfect, deep, and dream-filled sleep;
Yet spying her, a Man stopped in his tracks,
And soon she wished his mortal heart to keep.
Nefandous dreams and maddening nightmare
Were what she must endure their lives to share.

A SORCERESS'S LOVE

His eyes of ebony ensnare
Even the bravest Amazon.
His charms, a gift, the devil's share,
Rival the radiance of dawn.

My circle drawn, my life-blood spilt,
I call my incubus most fair.
In glowing embers, darkest silt,
Appears he in the smoky air.

Such fire I taste upon my lips,
Yet it's his touch that is divine!
No sin has ever tempted trips
Into the void to get what's mine.

Such venom taints his serpent tongue,
But oh it is the taste I crave!
His claws so ache to tear my lung,
Yet for his touch I'll risk my grave.

He is the cosmic storm, its rage;
The swirling night and its abyss.
He is the Chaos and its sage,
My daemon and my sinful bliss.

I am his Circe; he, my love;
My pet no other mistress claims.
He comes, for there's no force above
That can defeat our hearts' twin flames.

A Lover's Sorceress

Her eyes were of a green witch-fire
Like carven emeralds agleam.
Her painted lips, a purple mire,
Enchanted me like depths of dream.

Across the void she summons me,
And ever must I heed her call.
I am her slave to never flee,
For in this ring, I'm in her thrall.

Her languid gaze allures me near,
Yet her enchanted ring holds fast.
She teases as she, without fear,
Draws near to her salt circle cast.

Her breaths of belladonna waft
Through velvety envenomed lips.
Her alabaster form, so soft
Beneath her robe, is in my grips.

I take her in my arms, yet her
Enchantments shield her from all harm.
My touch will ever make her purr,
Yet I am captured by her charm!

She is the twilight, its illusion
Of day and night that blend in haze.
She is the Seer in her seclusion,
My sorceress and worth my praise.

I am her daemon; she, my lover,
She, vicious sorceress of mine.
A fiend a human form can't cover,
A goddess worthy of a shrine.

PANIC

The emerald glen, agleam with light
That falls through arms of trees,
Lies cool and soft beneath the flight
Of nymphs and fae that tease.

The shepherd lusts for honey sweet
That no sweet flower sates,
And yearns for cherries ripe to eat
From such succulent mates.

His horns reach high above his mane,
Which flows in long brown locks;
His phallus aches to play and drain
Inside Bacchantic flocks.

The great god Pan can panic strike
Inside the hearts of men
And creatures, till his pleasure spike
Wanes—then he waits again.

A song of honeyed verse flows through
The meadows, and the scent
Of lilac billows past the yew—
She was of nymph descent.

She was all his, in wildest dreams,
Fair shepherdess of lust.
He yearned to hear her moans and screams—
But Syrinx showed disgust.

He offered then to bless her sheep
With twins for every spring,
For just one night with her to reap
His pleasure from the fling.

His bold advances Syrinx shunned,
And she enflamed his rage.
He followed her and then he stunned
Her changing in the sage.

She changed herself to reeds to get
Away from him, and he
Destroyed the wood and his new pet
So she could never flee.

He made a pretty pipe with her
Now broken, tattered form,
And her sweet song is now a slur
Like music from a storm.

His love was faithless for the dame,
Yet she remained with him
In jagged lengths all much the same,
And ever played his hymn.

Fair Syrinx, her most lovely voice
Shrieks ever through the pipe
Of her new master without choice—
Pan took her in one swipe.

A panic pierces through the night
In those who do not heed
Pan's strong desires for those in flight;
Submit to him or bleed.

MAENADS

Beneath the sky the posies sway
To dancing maenads' beat.
They spend their lovers in their play,
And taste of their sweet meat.

In sarcoline and clinging silks,
They tease the eyes of men.
The men drip seed like freshest milks,
Releasing lust they pen.

Each man will sweat to please his nymph,
Though mortal men will match
Few tastes as satyr blood and lymph—
Yet men are quick to catch!

A night of fire, a night of bliss,
Yet dawn comes to them all.
Their breath bequeathed by one last kiss,
They please and then they fall.

"In sarcoline and clinging silks,
They tease the eyes of men."

THEY SING IN WHISPERS

Eburnean, his horns reach to the sky,
Toward the star-filled vault; his ever sly,
Enchanting grin strays slightly longer when
His devilish and hungry gaze sees skin
Of the most luscious nymphs, with flesh like silk
Of ebony or that of freshest milk.
Great Pan, the god of shepherds, god of flocks,
Becks like a siren to the maids he stalks.
He craves the tastes of honeyed tongues and lips
Of cherries red and ripe wherein he slips
In with the passion of a god of lust.
His emerald eyes—inspiring dim mistrust,
Yet perfect rapture!—lure the purest rose
To dances faster, faster! till they're close
To moaning forth his name from tainted tongues.
They sing in whispers, loosing from their lungs
A sated sigh as they lie spent, alone.
For Syrinx he would stay—yet she has flown.

A GLAMOROUS TOUCH

I lie unmoving deep inside a dream;
I wake abruptly, bathed in moon's cold light.
The window's vista almost makes me scream:
My heart aches crimson—for he's now in sight!
Near in an instant, my dark prince, my knight!
Transfixed upon him, I stand petrified.
Embracing me, he takes the fatal bite. . . .
Becoming wan and weak, I sting inside.

His kiss awakes sensations I can't hide—
His sanguine smirk enflames me in his clutch.
Once he releases, standing by my side,
My love ignites—so glamorous, his touch!
But he won't make me his nocturnal kin,
For nightly teasing is his sweetest sin.

PRISONER OF LOVE

A surly, sweet caress will sate the needs
Of primal urges, yet it will not mask
The quiet dangers that a dungeon breeds . . .
For little sunlight shines where I can bask.
Just when the moon is high and starlets play
Does comes my captor to indulge his taste.
I am a slave of love, though why, I say,
When sets the sun, do I so mourn his haste?

ON AMARANTHINE LIPS

My purple font of his desire
Invites the tongue of my vampire.
He tastes the nectar sweet therein,
And drinks his fill of darkest sin.
His kiss on amaranthine lips
Delivers bliss down to my hips.
Forever his caress is cold,
Yet how I itch for him to hold
Me in his arms, for every star
Above to see us from afar.

Sweet Renegade

Sweet renegade so fair, eternal, true,
Your heart grows vibrant when I am with you.
Your burning lips of red don't hide such lies;
The truth allures me from behind those eyes.
The rarest breed her kin descended from—
The wicked sirens, whisper not just some.
The singing vixens pull my taut heartstrings,
Yet obvious disdain this siren brings.
Her seething rage shows suddenly above,
Yet underneath it all, she fears true love.
Her weakness just for me enflames her so;
Her hate for weakness makes my love just grow.
She ceased her song in hope to find the cure
To the pursuit, yet that was the allure.
I am not human, yet their ways of love
Made me desirous of a life above.
She left her kind who dwell in the cold sea
To run away from the suave likes of me.
She mixed with mortals at a Samhain ball,
And chatted freely, talking to them all.
Her voice, however, never will be free
Of her alluring tone, which called to me.
The faint attraction I've been searching for
Has led me straight to the loquacious floor.
The ladies ravenously hint for fun—
And yet my eyes are set on only one.
My fine appearance has caused quite a spell,
Yet I am here for just the ball's fair Belle.

Encircled by a dashing entourage,
She then is offered many a corsage.
Each trying failingly to capture her,
Only I know what makes her heart to stir.
First they all shift their eyes in my direction,
Abruptly threatened by my keen inspection.
All movement ceased, their muscles quickly strain—
She turns to gaze at her daemonic swain.
I arrogantly smirked from ear to ear,
Then suddenly she felt devoid of fear.
With silent strides, I closed the glitzy distance.
When near to her, she ceased her coy resistance.
Then, as the ball became a sudden blur,
I found my voice and spoke so soft to her:
'You're bound to me, my sweet, sweet renegade,
So please don't stop your luring serenade.'

Siren's Song

O siren song, just sing to me;
Enchant my soul, for I am yours.
Just never quit your melody,
For through my beating heart it pours.

Your touch sends many strange sensations
Throughout my warm and tender core.
Who knew Hell offered such temptations
To make me ache to be so sore?

She swims the white and frigid river,
And beckons as she leads the way.
One step—I falter and I shiver;
It's then that I begin to sway.

Her dark enchantment cast a spell
I cannot break—I cannot win.
Beneath her power, where I dwell,
I only serve, and feed her sin.

SEPHORA

The lovat pool produced soft ripples from her touch.
The water clung to her yet did not hide too much.
Her skin was pale and glistened like rose-petals white
And dipped in dew from charming flowers of the night.
She was as lovely as a chatelaine from great
Intriguing castles from Averoigne of late.
She was a stranger though, to this time and these lands,
For far beyond this realm, her ancient kingdom stands.

Sephora was her name, Enchantress of renown
In Sylaire, her high kingdom, where she holds the crown.
Through paths that serpentined through the dry antique wood
She saw the falling suns and rising moons and stood
At the threshold to her domain, her realm of charms.
Her magic blocked her home from those who'd stand at arms,
Yet a hermit of such fine handsome features like
Anselme, would be so hard to refuse for spikes
Arose inside her darkened heart at his sweet glance.
Perhaps this lusting lover will make her heart dance.

A wolf of deepest blacks and richest blues emerged
From lurking shadows eyeing the hermit and urged
Him, with hot eyes of gold, to stray not from her grasp.
The wolf, or maybe a true Were, began to rasp;
Its lolling tongue gave forth the savor of a root
Unknown to Anselme, some herb of ill repute.
Yet Sephora, a great enchantress, cares not for
What the hermit soon thinks or hears of Sylaire's lore.

Enchantress of aeons, fair Sephora arose
To gaze upon her catch from her window and froze.
Her ancient lover, wolf of wolves, transformed to man
In front of her new guest and spoke of some strange plan.
She knew inside, he would give the Mirror of Truth
To her hermit and would reveal then her false youth!
She waited for him to come and he soon arrived
In bloody rags so caked with fur and scars, yet thrived.
He held up the mirror and threw it in the burs
And then embraced her and she knew, he was all hers.

—After Clark Ashton Smith's "The Enchantress of Sylaire"

CAN I STOP YOUR HEART?

Even in rapture, I will not see you—
My love for you dissolved to dust within.
How can I stop your heart, is it a sin?
My love is gone, which time cannot undo.
My feelings for you are no longer true;
Your soul rings out, yet I can't hear the din.
Your heart-strings are still strong, yet mine are thin—
Mine strum with sorrow, I am filled with rue.

Yet opportunity always awaits. . . .
Don't waste your heart on love at any cost—
For lightning strikes outside of Hell's cold gates,
Releasing incubi from out the frost.
New love will soon rekindle your burnt heart,
And then a perfect rapture will restart.

ENTRY FOUR:
ON A DREAMLAND'S MOON

DAEMONOLATRY

Elysian daemon worship is more than it seems,
For many fiends reside in the deep haunted reaches
Of our vast psyche. Shun them, and they escape through dreams.
Approach them with respect; wait what the daemon teaches. . . .

GOETIA

Sigils, black signs, and carved archaic symbols
With offerings of blood pricked with cold wimbles,
May grant you audience with a dark knight.
Or maybe you'll call forth an earl tonight.
A scent of myrrh and Saturn rule above
Your knights, and maybe you will earn their love
With gifts of air, their seals inscribed in black.
Beware, for if you leave your circle-track
Your magic shield deserts you; and without
Their own triangle, you'll be theirs to flout.
If you should dare to aim a little higher,
The blood of dragons must perfume the fire.
Expelling spicy, copper-tainted fumes,
The dragon's breath pervades, convolves, consumes
The air, preparing for its honored earl,
Who soon appears in fumes, a smoky swirl.
Daemons will grant you kindness in return;
For just the same, without it, you shall burn.
Crude lead and copper only go so far,
For only gold and silver raise the bar.
Open your Goetia and all you seek
Will be inside to help you reach your peak.
No need to wait to meet that squamose prince;
Summon him by yourself—try not to wince.
Or is it a marquis that you require?
Perhaps it is a king you so desire?
Such worm-appendaged presidents will show
Unfathomable wonders, all they know,

If you are worth their wisdom and their time.
Insult or disrespect them—it's a crime
In their all-seeing eyes—and grim damnation
Or death await you, barring all salvation.
They all await your call, but for a price—
Without the proper gifts, they won't play nice.

THE BLACK GODDESS

O sweetest night, O mother of my soul,
Bestow upon me your benighted kiss!
What shadows shroud you from my midnight stroll?
What lurks unseen beneath your veils that hiss?

Asteria, what omens have you seen
Bedecked upon the welkin's falling stars?
What visions have you glimpsed in Algol's green
Irradiance oft witnessed from afar?

O Nyx, what secrets do you hide within,
Which even mighty Zeus may fear from you?
What lies behind your sempiternal grin?—
Forbidden knowledge that I wish I knew!

Fair Nótt, you ride the chariot that brings
The night across all kingdoms, but what of
Yet still another darkness, one with wings,
Which carries blackened secrets from above?

O primal goddess Nu, what darksome grace
From watery depths of an unknown abyss
Will you bestow upon the depths of space?
What life will you create with one dark kiss?

What flowers perilous have been plucked dry
To aid a magic spell to make me numb?
The mist of death will shroud my eyes, and I
Will know, my dear Achlys, that you have come.

O blackened goddess, my eternal night,
On this benighted path I follow now,
Please be my guide, extinguish all my light!
My blood shall spill for this nocturnal vow.

—Inspired by Richard Gavin's *The Benighted Path*

LIGEIA

I cannot summon the old memory of when
I first became acquainted with her, yet since then
I have long felt that we have never been apart.
Her form of sculpted marble, lips of reddest heart,
Her voice of sweetest song, and eyes of fondest dreams,
Allured my heart of hearts—her face forever beams.
Her face, no maiden matched, for she was wildly fine;
Her skin rivaled the purest ivory of the Rhine.

Ligeia was her name, belovèd wife of mine.
She fell violently prey to vultures such that dine
And thrive on flights of passion, which I could not measure,
Except by her fierce rapture from wild words of pleasure.
She grew ill, though her eyes blazed with effulgence still;
Yet her pale fingers turned a waxen hue to chill
The very heart of me, and I knew she would die.
She wrestled greatly with the Shadow that was nigh;
And as I sat beside her, she poured out her heart
To me with words of love to match a poet's art.

I knelt beside her ebon bed and spoke a verse
To her, yet soon, how soon, she fell to Death's cold curse!
I crushed into the very ground with sorrow's weight,
And held it long with me though even timely Fate
Would grant another wife to me, for she was not
Ligeia, and I loathed her with a hate that ought
To burn within a daemon rather than in me.
She too fell ill while I knelt near upon one knee.

She spoke of sounds and motions, yet I could not hear,
Could not see; and as time went on, she pressed this fear.
In her, a deadly pallor spread, and I sought wine;
Yet as she drank, three phantom drops fell in, in line.
A faint, soft shadow of such cherubic contour
Just passed me by, and then, my wife was just no more!
I sat alone with her now shrouded form, and yet
I heard the sighs of breath and sounds I can't forget.
She rose from bed and shook the fetters off of Death—
The shroud fell off—Ligeia stood again with breath!

—After Edgar Allan Poe's "Ligeia"

GHOUL MISTRESS

One winter night I caught a glimpse of her.
Enwrapped in fog of ghostly, glowing green,
She followed in my wake, unheard, unseen.
Her icy, killing kisses had no cure.

She caught my eye and left the other fools,
For she had found the lover she desired.
Her eyes entrapped me, and I was admired;
I was her mortal, diamond of her jewels.

She drifted through the fog and drew so near,
Admiring me with greenish goblin-fires.
Without a word, she knew my dark desires;
She could unlock my most forbidden fear.

Before I said a single word, she kissed
My lips and stirred a storm of ice in me.
My skin grew cold, yet, dying, I was free.
My ghoulish mistress only would be missed.

MY CORPSE, MY GROOM

In eldritch crypts, beneath acidic stars,
My corpse, my groom, in pieces lies in wait
For my endearing touch to heal his scars.
Yet it's my sun-kissed flesh that has of late
Turned white as moons; it's my eyes that have sunk
To deathly gray; and it's my hunger that
Has taken over; for I need to dunk
My fingertips into his flesh, his fat.
My ghoulish kiss will taste his lips once more—
And yet his heart's the treat I'm longing for.

A Valkyrie's Vendetta

A goddess filled with strong vitality,
She lost her life by fierce brutality.
Her soul reborn, her body still was not;
Bewitched, a walking corpse she was soon wrought.
A demigoddess, servitor of slain
And fallen warriors, she crossed the plain.
A vast unkindness of haematic ravens
Arose to feast as spirits reached their havens.
With icy eyes and lips of deep poinsettia,
A hatred fed a Valkyrie's vendetta.
Her beauty, broken by Death's frigid touch,
Forever rotted, was in Odin's clutch.
Fair Freyja sternly stated that she earn
The cherished youthful looks for which she yearned.
Yet mead-hall maiden she refused to be—
She would enjoy one day a killing spree.
With her as ruler as in life's dim past,
She could attain her glory at long last.

THE ROTTING GODDESS

Her armor casts auroras through the sky
When she goes riding through the fields of slain
And fallen fighters, yet they all must die
By her enchanting hands, they fight in vain.

Her reddened fingertips pluck at the strings
Of the intestines strung throughout her loom.
She weaves the fates of fighting men and kings
While severed heads are hanging in the gloom.

The twelve vile valkyries weave swiftly in
The favor of their champions, or they
Cast vicious curses 'gainst their foes to win.
The rotting goddesses choose whom to slay.

"Her reddened fingertips pluck at the strings
Of the intestines strung throughout her loom."

NYARLATHOTEP

I am the Crawling Chaos and I am the last.
From twenty-seven centuries of nighted past
I rise, receiving messages not of this plane.
Across the lands I enter, screams and chaos reign,
So that the pallid moon pities and frowns upon
The crumbling towns my presence brings, till all is gone.

—After H. P. Lovecraft's "Nyarlathotep"

ON A DREAMLAND'S MOON

The cats of Ulthar steal across my dreams
On paws of softest fur and blur the seams
Of my subconscious with their purrs and eyes
Of molten gold that twinkle and that gleam
Like beacon lights toward where their kingdom lies.
I dream a dreamer's dream of longing for
Entrance to Dreamland and the moon's closed doors.
Nyarlathotep, the God of Chaos, soon
Awaits in dream; for him, my heart outpours!
Why must He lurk afar, behind cursed rune?
The ghouls repeat his words, "I am the last,
I am the Crawling Chaos. From long past
Centuries, I hear words not of this plane.
Renewing myths from times far gone, I cast
Chaos across the lands—Chaos will reign."
The pixie parasols of royal blues
Bedecked the path to doors of vibrant hues.
I had to follow it and try to see
My emperor of dreams, for all rare views
Of him would scarcely answer my dark plea!
The hallways luminous began to dim,
And as I entered the next room, the grim
Expressions of distracted Lengish men
Upon me looked, as moon-beasts with wet limbs
And grayish skin gazed eyeless through the den.
The coiling lurkers in the serpent-pools
Appeared to hint with their black socket-jewels
Of some excitement imminent, and held

The men of Leng back, for they would be fools
To spoil my hunt to find where my king dwelled.
A snicker echoed through my head, and I
Knew that my god was watching with keen eye.
O how I shivered for His very touch!
I offered up my mind—for me to die
Would lend a soul unworthy of His clutch.
Hot are the sands of time, yet on I tread,
For every step I take ignites my red
And pumping heart aflame with a desire
For Him, my god, to pull my heartstrings' thread.
My trembling thighs grow moist from no sand's fire.

Hail Nitokris, my patron, grant me skill
In amorous endeavors so the thrill
Of His enchantment will coil round my soul!
O queen of ghouls, O goddess of the kill,
Adorn me with the power of your whole
Being; instill in me the strength beyond
My mortal kin! My madness makes a bond
With you and, surely, Him . . . O please be so!
In swirls of yellow does my queen respond
And give to me her maddened blessing, though
Will it enough be for my lord, my king?
Nyarlathotep, he speaks—yet will He sing?—
Into my ears soft words that vanish like
The sand through fingers; like the chill in spring.
He is aware of me yet will not strike.

"Within my crimson-teared and flaming eyes!
My soul, now His, by His dire hand was felled."

* * *

My god has come to me in dreams with sweet
And feverous desires released in heat.
His hands upon me set my skin aflame,
And lingering, His taste is still a treat
Upon my lips; His tongue begins to claim
The contours of my torso, hips, and thighs.
He calls to me; I come beneath the skies
Of poison reds, and fiery greens, and stars
That ever bleed upon these Dreamland sties.
Chaotic wasteland welcomes me, and scars
My mind like verse engraved on graveyard stone.
Up marble stairs and over ashen bone,
I start to hasten through the labyrinth's green
And yellow passages of star-dust, blown
Through the high windows, open wide, which glean
The stuff of star-winds in this land of dreams.
The walls with faceless souls pulse at the seams
Where they would claw their way through the gray walls.
They cry in direst warning, yet their screams
Are echoless, and I ignore their squalls.
The night-gaunts stalk me stealthily, unseen
In crevices above; with senses keen
They know my presence, swift reflections from
Their rubber wings betraying their black sheen.
They hunger for me, yet they will not come.
I enter the last chamber high inside
The palace where He waits for me beside

A window looking over Dreamland's moon.
He slightly turns his head toward his bride,
And fully faces me—O how I swoon!

I stood before the pharaoh darkly masked,
And I was lost in pride as the quest tasked
Me finally our meeting did allow!
"O love, will you unmask for me?" I asked.
His laughter echoed as He clutched his brow. . . .
A sinister abyss awaited my
Awestruck and hungry gaze, yet I did cry
Aloud, for Beauty itself I beheld
Within my crimson-teared and flaming eyes!
My soul, now His, by His dire hand was felled.
The Crawling Chaos stripped the flesh away
From my frail mortal husk, and the decay
Began to set in; and yet I was shown
Behind the mask as He beheld his prey.
The laughter grew, only it was my own.

NITOKRIS

Beneath the yawning gateways, underneath the last,
Third Pyramid, the ghoul-queen sleeps within the vast,
Nethermost onyx temple, in the void below.
She sleeps amid rich gems, untouched by sunlight's glow,
And with the mummies that are neither man nor beast.
Still living, she was buried for a deadly feast. . . .
Some shun her Pyramid beneath Egyptian moons—
Queen Nitokris was legend 'mid the desert dunes.

The great Sixth Dynasty portrayed a nymph in youth—
How easily she lured her foes in peace; in truth,
She offered them unto the Nile and drowned them all
By throwing wide the water-gates in Temple Hall.
Her cachinnation echoed still as she was thrown
Into her grand sarcophagus of golden stone.
She lies there with Him of the Sphinx, as tales were told—
He of the Second Pyramid, Khephren of old.
So far beneath the ground, he wed the ghoulish queen,
And with her ruled over the mummies, vaguely seen.

The horrors Egypt hides endure in olden tombs,
Where phantom priest-processions still disperse the fumes
Of richest resins as they offer up their gods
Unspeakable, dread sacrifice impaled on rods.
The mummies without souls and hordes of devil-cursed
Pharaonic dead and restless kas know wicked thirst
Amid the onyx darkness of the queen and king.
The queen awaits whatever desert sands may bring.

The stone colossi marched in endless night and drove
The herds of grinning androsphinxes down a cove
To shores of stagnant rivers, black as pitch and cold.
It was her necromancy that called through the hold
To lure the dead and servants there so she could steal
The spirits out of victims lost and make them kneel
Before her as sweet sacrifices or new slaves.
Yet each new offering would fall unto their graves
If they should merely glimpse her visage, for the fools
Would see her face was gnawed by rats and starving ghouls.

—After H. P. Lovecraft's "Under the Pyramids"

Diary of a Sorceress

WINTER WITCH

In crystal towers lit by silver moons,
The winter witch invokes the Holly King.
Into the world, she casts with ancient runes
A velvet darkness from which he will spring.

She shuns the sun the Oak King conjures now,
And exiles him to the abyss beyond.
She bleeds the flesh of her silk wrist in vow
To fell the sun above and seal the bond.

THE NECRO-CONJURING SORCERESS

The necro-conjurer, a sorceress of zeal,
Could feel the chill of night that crept throughout her lair.
So intricate her make, as cold and hard as steel,
That even the cadaver, well preserved with care,
Was not more icy than her sinister embrace.
Her silken skin delivered forth the final touch
To his last memories that soon she must erase.
With kisses, he again was in her deadly clutch;
She killed her lover out of great and envious rage.
His cloudy eyes wide opened, first beholding her.
Her scent, desirable, intoxicating sage,
Awoke a distant vision—it was but a blur.
With runic ritual, and ancient spoken spell,
She overtook his body and his weakened mind.
With hunger now for humans, he was bound for Hell,
And a new target came, to rip and have confined.

The jealous Sorceress had found his love untrue,
For he was found to have a mistress wyrding-skilled.
The mistress proved too hard to easily subdue,
So uttered she a spell so cruel and darkly willed.
She turned to face her shameful love who begged and knelt,
But she could feel no pity for dishonored trust.
To kill him was a simple justice to be dealt;
He knew his end would come by unrestrainèd lust.
With magic-powered strength, she dragged his cold remains
Into her lonely tower in the haunted wood.
Preserved and prepped to soon arise upon this plane,

He would perforce obey her, and he understood.
The Sorceress caressed his pallid chest with sharp
And blackened fingertips one final time ere she
Became ensanguined, plucking tendons like a harp.
She stilled his heart to silence for all time his plea.

Malicious feelings set his dull, dim mind aflame,
Not only for the taste of luscious human flesh,
But to appease the Sorceress in her vile game,
And feel the life drain out of someone still so fresh.
His mistress was the single craving that he sought
With such a teasing image pictured in his head—
He wanted nothing but to watch her slowly rot,
Then feast upon her entrails till her corpse lay dead.

The Sorceress just stood and watched her precious pet,
Just like the proudest mother watches children grow.
He rose frustrate by stiffness, but he shuffling set
Toward his pulsing prey through the harsh wind and snow.
He left her high witch-tower and she closed her eyes
Awaiting the most savage of unearthly cues;
The silence shattered at the mistress' last cries;
The Sorceress grinned widely, knowing she was through.

Narda the Czarina

Above the town of Halycz lay a slave
On lavish folds of silk, who darkly gave
Her master languid stares beneath black lashes.
An ample garment of dark silks and sashes,
A coat of somber fur, enveloped her;
A creature, ravishing, beneath the fur.
Her tresses fell in reddened rows of coral,
And her alluring features shamed the floral
Décor, all while her darkened eyes agleam
Flamed like chimeras born of heated dream.
Her czar, so virile, vowed on bended knee
That she would rule him and his kingdom, free
Of bondage for a day, with him for slave.
She took her place upon the throne and gave
Her lover, once the czar, one chance to please
Her, letting slip her scarlet dress to tease. . . .
A Goddess, as impassive and as cold,
Revealed to her tormented love of old
Her succulent and luscious shapes of pure
Divinity, him dumb with her allure.
The Black Czarina cracked her whip in rage,
And lashed his face as if he were a page!
The czar then pressed his dry, enfevered lips
Against her foot, ere axe's black eclipse.

—After Leopold von Sacher-Masoch's *The Black Czarina*

CASTLE CSEJTHE

In corridors of stone, the claws of girls engrave
The walls with horizontal marks of darkest red.
The blood and broken nails embed and paint, then pave
The way toward the torture chambers, realms of dread.

The pallid ladies, beautiful as ocean's foam,
Were playthings of the Countess, and their prizèd blood
Flowed forth like to a crimson sea, where she would comb
Her hair with it or bathe beneath its endless flood.

In castle Csejthe, hell awaits those maidens pure
Of heart and pure of mind, for Bathory desires
Them both. She steals their very breath to find a cure
For even death, till life eternal she acquires!

PAINTED IN BLOOD

The countess had a corpse from every home
In her high court of maiden blood and bone.
The freshest flower spurts the sweetest foam;
She savored every drop…and every moan.

No courtly daughter or shy peasant maid
Escaped her deadly pleasures and her ploys.
Their every scream was music to be swayed
From their cracked lips; their bodies were her toys.

She combed her hair with shards of pallid teeth,
And washed away, with tortured tears, the mud.
She dressed in crimson robes, and yet beneath,
Her marble skin was painted red with blood.

"She dressed in crimson robes, and yet beneath,
Her marble skin was painted red with blood."

BATHORY IN RED

Her reddened fingertips embed
Themselves in flesh of dames.
Her reddened tongue has licked and bled
Dry nobles; doused like flames.

Her reddened lips have sucked and kissed
And tasted the life out
Of peasants not so sorely missed.
Their blood pours like a spout.

As pale as moons, her aging skin
Is reddened by slit throats
And gaping, ever gaping grins.
In baths of blood, she gloats.

I. NADIA

Bright flames of scarlet licked the midnight sky
In twirling tendrils so like silky curls.
Her tresses whipped against the pale of pearls—
Her skin the wind exposed as she drew nigh
The castle gates, whose gargoyles towered high
Like awful forms of daemon knights and earls.
Her lustrous eyes were lit like moon-gray whorls
Amid the darkness and the wind's weird sigh.

Dark Nadia, wicked countess of the dead,
Traveled to far-off lands so she could sample
The many tastes and finer shades of red
That hotly dripped from necks beneath her trample.
She loved with such a venomous love of pain
And mischief which had driven her insane.

II. BAT IN THE BOILER ROOM

Obtenebration of the lone black bat,
Though tiny, flickered, twirled, as flames let fly
Defiant embers at stone walls nearby.
The boiler room was lit; the hallways sat
So desolate, the darkness leering at
The creature who leered back, its pledge held high;
Unknown to most, still strong its ancient tie.
He waited for his Countess, that was that.

He waited in still solitude to find
That whispers hissed from some exotic land.
Above the nighted wood that mountains lined,
In haunting grandeur did the castle stand.
Beyond the halls invisible in gloom,
The bat hung waiting in the boiler room.

III. Black Orchid

A darkness drifts in wisps like thick black smoke
As she, the Countess, leaves behind the town
And dull mundane that always made her frown.
What does she care if one mere man should croak?
Fair Nadia rolled her moon-gray eyes and spoke:
'A fairer man than this one, who did drown,
Would not have let his blood besmear my gown
Before I left him in the brine to choke.'

She held a lone black orchid in her hand
As she proceeded back to her fine home.
The note and blossom were left on her stand
Unnoticed as she watched a man from foam
And sea lie bloodless in his final hole.
She read it, clutching to her heart the scroll.

IV. THE POWER OF THE SUN

She was so young when he defeated her.
A mighty warrioress she was, and yet,
Centuries old, he won all wars he met.
The fatal bite of death left all a blur.
His fragrance sweetened her descent, for myrrh
Was soothing while she saw her last sunset.
She soon awoke in shadows, crawling jet,
And yet her tainted heart no more would stir.

Her skin reflected now the pale starlight,
And irises once sapphire turned moon-gray.
Infinitely afflicted by his bite,
She turned into a vampyress to prey
Upon mankind, though one dear star would shun
Her for all time; she could not face the sun.

BLOOD SIREN'S ALCOVE

The scarlet-painted scallops lined the walls
Anear dead sailors lured there by her calls.
The walls of bone and abalone formed
Her sunken alcove, whose dark chamber swarmed
With merfolk freshly killed, and human fools.
Their blood ensanguined angel-wings and jewels
From pearl-creating oysters, bits of shell.
When tides recede, her pool's a bloody well,
And she awaits the next providing wave
That brings new sailors near her song. They crave
The lovely courtship she implies, and yet
Their quick arrival they too soon regret.

ANTHROPOMANCY

His flesh was marble, sculpted to perfection, and his eyes
Were opals crystalline like those in ancient dragon hoards.
When first she saw him, she made sure he fell for her sweet lies,
And then he followed her to her black tower above the fjords.

With venomous affections and her poison-filled white wine,
She danced with her desirous paramour till death had seeped
Into his heated form, and waited till she could divine. . . .
Silence soon settled, for her lovers corpses heaped and heaped.

The now sweet, tantalizing ichor from his flesh still young
Ensnared her senses, and with each caress of his stiff member,
She fell for sins of flesh, his taste still fresh on her forked tongue.
Her trophy coldly lay, and yet her eyes lit up like embers!

She passionately stroked his pale chest down to his abdomen,
And felt his skin, so soft beneath her blackened fingertips.
With cravings succubi can match, she sought to find the omen
He held inside, and with her knife, she plunged in to the grip.

From palest blue to ruby red, he lay obedient
And quiet as his Sorceress so gingerly took parts
Away and pulled his entrails out—the sole ingredient
For true anthropomancy, her prized form of the black arts.

Diary of a Sorceress

CARATHIS

Her skin of burnished bronze, so silken to the touch;
Her hair of blackest midnight, wafting scents of such
Intoxicating aphrodisiacs; and her
Enticing eyes of hazel that made weak hearts stir,
Belonged to the dark Sorceress of high Samarah.
Fools only would court this dark queen whose mouth is marah.
Her heart was ice within a cage of blackened bone.
Carathis was her name, and she would rule alone.

Inside the high witch-tower of her dark delights,
She decked her walls with hanging bodies all alight.
Her floors were red, her followers were all deaf mutes,
And mummies who attended to her brews of newts.
Emitting fumes of mummies and the blazing flames
Frequently filled her working space as, without shame,
She practiced rituals, with offerings spread out.
Her tainted mind had found for certain, without doubt,
An entrance to the Palace of Subterranean Fire.
A place of treasures and rare knowledge to desire.

Such sacrifices of serpents and scorpions
Soon insufficient grew, and fresh new champions
Were needed to appease her gods of pain and death.
Servants, friends, children were the same, for every breath
Could easily be stilled, for passage down below.
Reciting savage incantations soon let go
Her earthly limits, and she entered down with bliss
Into the palace where, awaiting, was Eblis.

He greeted her as newly hired within his ranks,
And offered food and wine, which eagerly, she drank.
He gave free range of his grand palace, and she soon
Surveyed every dark corridor. How she did swoon
When finally she came upon her long sought prize:
The talismans of Soliman that held the skies
And conquered all beneath them! Quickly grabbing one,
Her heart burst into flames with a heat like the sun!
Explosive cachinnation pierced the many halls
As her shrill screams forever echoed in his walls.

—After William Beckford's *Vathek*

TWISTED TRAILS OF THOUGHT

For K. A. O.

Amid the shadows of a tavern brightly lit,
Where boastful bards are singing horrid songs with wit,
There sits a silent bard alone, who sips his drink
While contemplating how those poetasters stink. . . .

Unlike those bards who sing their songs of bygone valor—
Ardent, with reddened cheeks—this bard of spectral pallor
Inscribes in blood so sinister a literature
Of such nefandous depths, and yet of such allure.

Deep twisted trails of thought stream through his darksome mind,
Full of cacodaemonic tales, and spells that bind.
A fresh, alluring corpse, a lovely, ruined heart—
These fill the caverns of his soul and never part.

The blackest thoughts course through his magic fingertips,
And through his ceremonial work, nightmare soon grips.
His dark and intricate delights are spells he crafts,
Which summon shivers and cold shakes from more than drafts.

His art boasts of itself without the need for speech—
His poems touch deep places that so few can reach.
Such weaker bards all harbor secret fear of him;
Their thoughts, in public, never could be quite so grim.

LADY IN BLACK VELVET

They danced in whirls of color on the ballroom floor,
Until the black-gowned Lady of the Masque of lore.
Did enter like a wintry dream, with stately air,
So richly, gravely dressed with skin so pale and fair.
Her entrance caused a stir, and yet her cold eyes fell
Upon my ward and me, who fell beneath her spell.
The music, instrumentals of exquisite song,
Did echo through the lamp-lit grounds the whole night long.
The fireworks were unlike all Paris past had seen,
And yet she in the long black velvet stole the scene.
The lady, an obsidian 'mid chalcedon,
Was whispered of, and to her I was strangely drawn.
She soon entranced me with her words, alluding to
Our past engagements, long forgotten till she drew
Them out from my faint memory with her mere touch.
She parried my attempts to find out just as much
As her fair name, yet did it pleasantly and sweet.
Yet her appearance hinted toward a dark deceit,
For she took an unnatural delight in my
Uneasiness, as my attempts did fail to pry
From her vermilion lips a clue of any kind.
A clock abruptly tolled, she left, yet not from mind.
Now that her spell unwove, I wondered at her threat;
The lady in black velvet I had never met.

—After J. Sheridan Le Fanu's "Carmilla"

MIRCALLA

The faintest wind from out the east so softly steals
Across the lands of Styria, Hell on its heels.
The palest maiden of the darkest hair of brown,
And languid eyes of deep allure to surely drown
The weakest hearts, arose from out the fallen wreckage
And just emerging roots that overturned her carriage.
Yet with the shock, a faint ensued—the maiden fell.
She would be cared for, yet they were beneath her spell.

Carmilla was her name, and though she seemed as sweet
As sunlight's kiss, to learn her secrets was a feat.
Her words were like soft lullabies adrift above,
And such entrapments made the foolish fall in love.
Yet her most silent secrets were more shrouded than
The whispers of the moon in evening's waning span.
Before the maid became a guest, an old nightmare
Emerged from memory in which she strove to snare
The senses of fair Laura, lady of the schloss—
Yet that was surely fancy; she would not be cross.

The moon that night was full of such odylic charm;
How could its silver radiance observe such harm?
Decay and death ensued across the nearby town,
Yet death brought not a crease unto Carmilla's crown.
Her midnight disappearances, she claimed, were walks
In sleep, yet she could not account for all the locks.
A weakness grew from needle-pricks in Laura's breast,
And a suspicion lurked and hinted toward their guest. . . .

"The axe was raised; her scream came forth, all filled with dread.
The axe then fell and she was silenced, she was dead."

Accompanied by a true friend, the lord and Laura
Abruptly trekked toward the plains of stone and flora.
The very last of countesses would have been buried
In tombs beneath the chapel whereto they were carried:
The Ruins of Karnstein, rumored grave of fine Mircalla.
The countess, sly as snakes and swift as the impala,
Lay as if fast asleep, and realization struck—
Their guest lay in dull marble, bathed in crimson muck!
The axe was raised; her scream came forth, all filled with dread.
The axe then fell and she was silenced, she was dead.

—After J. Sheridan Le Fanu's "Carmilla"

WITH A LOVE SO VILE

For D. L. Myers

The Oracle treads the land with grace and stealth.
Remnants of mist trail fleetingly away
As, nourishing the nightshade blooms in wealth,
At night he waits for a life to decay.
Few silver strands of wisdom touch his face
As claws of wind wisp by that dare to play.
He is a man above the human race,
Yet his cold heart has found one like the fae.
And with a love so vile, so soon, he savors
Her sweetened torment and her screams like songs.
With matchless beauty, the great Oracle favors
Her pain to joy, until for death she longs.

THE EASTER LILY

The chorus from the wolves and crows
Echoes across the lake,
Where Easter lilies sway and shake
Beneath the bounding does.

Atop the waters, each twin sun
Reflects its sickly shades
Of orange and red till daylight fades
From wastes so drear and dun.

'Twas there, in lost Carcosa, where
His voice was said to swell
Through flaming lights of golden hell,
And fade to whispers fair.

It is a fearful thing to fall
Into the hands of Him;
The Living God, the maskless Grim,
The King in Yellow's thrall.

—Inspired by Robert W. Chambers and Ambrose Bierce

EVEN MADNESS CANNOT HIDE

The murmurs blow across the barren land
Of dim Carcosa, spoke from spectral lips.
A stillness wraps me with its wintry hands;
A strange awareness heightens, then it slips.

A weakness creeps and slithers deep inside,
From the foreboding presence of the King.
A torment even madness cannot hide
Arises, and I crave what Death would bring.

I kneel on bended knee and bow my head,
Yet such a power upward pulls my face.
I see behind the Pallid Mask, and red
And yellow fire engulfs me, from His Grace. . .!

The land is flooded by my wails and cries,
His voice triumphant in the flaming light.
His searing fire inflates to monstrous size
As I fall down the black abyss of night.

—After Robert W. Chambers's *The King in Yellow*

HORROR

In dark cathedrals and woodlands mist-laden,
A horror lurks in realms beyond, unseen.
Few fae are pretty and appear to maidens—
Most of their kind are cruel, and ugly green.

A door can lead to their true territory—
The Otherworld, where anyone might stray.
It changes Paradise to Purgatory,
And all cold shadows pave, for you, the way.

THE MEDALLION

It haunts me in my deepest dreams,
And ever lurks inside my head.
Its mazes lure, its silver gleams,
Its single gem is ever red.

The crimson gemstone pierces me
As if it stares into my soul.
The medallion is some cryptic key,
Yet I know not its hidden goal.

Diary of a Sorceress

ILVAA

The Silver Death, for now, has fled before this ring
Of strange red metal and black gems to suit a king.
The plague came down from Achernar, that brilliant star
That glares upon me without ceasing, from afar.
I am a realmless king with three surviving slaves,
And must in Cyntrom find my shelter, past the waves.
We crashed and then were captured by the island men.
That's when she came; and to their king they brought me then.

Her name was Ilvaa, and she wore vermillion skirts
And breast-cups of bright lazuli, fairest of flirts.
The dame upon me kindly smiled, yet led me to
The king of the dread Isle of Torturers and knew
That here I'd face my death instead of in my home.
The king sent me to rooms with views of ocean foam,
And devil-fish whose tentacles writhed on the walls,
And floating corpses, staring with their eyes' white balls.
With a soft haunting sorcery, her face returned.
For the first time in many suns, how my heart burned.

Aloft on his high brazen chair, the king sent me
To stand against grim torture without scarce a plea!
The fumes of dragon gall and the adipocere
Of long-dead cannibals were burned together here,
Intoxicating both my lungs and breathing-way.
Yet Ilvaa tenderly regarded me today,
And when the torture ceased, she crept into my room,
And twin desires of love and life began to bloom.

She silkily caressed my wet, enfevered brow,
And rubbed oils on my burning limbs with a stern vow
To set me free; and I believed her whispered word.
Yet dawn approached and she awaited with the herd,
And snickered without any shame as I was bound
Upon the wheel of adamant; her wine was browned
With poisons, yet her blackened lie was my true pain.
I begged to keep my ring—my trick was not in vain!
The king was quick to seize it and the Silver Death
Then came for me and them and it stilled every breath.

—After Clark Ashton Smith's "The Isle of the Torturers"

SATURN

The Lord of Time awaits inside His black
Tower of ice and malice, where the track
Of time allures Benighted kin to Him.
His jaws are seen in every grave, in grim
And gaping doorways, and strange haunted lands.
He feasts on all who stray into His hands.

—After Richard Gavin's *The Benighted Path*

VEXTERIA

The monoliths' reach upward stabs the purple sky
Like shadow claws that stretch in silence toward space.
Beneath them, in desert terrains, a loathsome race
Of creatures dwell beneath the searing sands, and spy.

The heavy storms of sand engulfed the planet once.
Oceans of cerulean became seas of sand.
The greatest cities turned to graveyards just as grand.
Few natives just escaped, all fleeing in response.

Aeons yet passed and evil poisoned their lush earth.
Strange skulls and polycephalic cadavers lay
Across hot plains and formed, as if they were soft clay,
Into great structures of some foul daemonic birth.

Arising in an amaranthine sky, the shrines
And temples ever leered with sharpened grins and gazed
With sightless sockets. Nothing could escape the maze
Of yellow scales and bones, and painted wings of wine.

Above, the natives watched the building up of bones,
And wondered if they were so built to worship them.
And yet no idols stood there, no religious gem
From Vexteria's lore. Their gods did not need thrones.

They worshiped gods from welkins past the horrid stars,
Beyond their poison rays, and once more will they come.
Vexteria is silent, save a vibrant hum
Caused by an unknown source, yet something not too far. . . .

A Sorceress's Final Vision

The icy moon above spilled light upon
Her skin of porcelain and lips of wine.
Her lavish locks of raven hair were drawn
Away in haste as she now searched her shrine
For signs of doom, yet they were quickly gone.

Her consecrated tools of such great power—
The chalice, wand, athame, and pentacle—
All failed the Sorceress in this late hour;
Anthropomancy, too, a spectacle
Even among grave robbers, had gone sour.

A horrid yet a fleeting glimpse of sights
Of burning reds aroused her from her sleep.
Remnants of it beplagued her like sharp bites
As on cold stones she hastened through her keep.

The phantom flames all vanished with a look;
Screams echoed down the empty corridors.
As she approached her dark, ensanguined book,
The fragments of the fleeting sight she bore
All disappeared; the text all blood had shook.

She scribed what little she remembered, yet
Her memories had vanished like stray wisps
Of mist that trailed away from dawn's dim threat
Of daylight warmth, which cut the clear night's crisp.

She stared upon her amethyst volume,
At such a loss as to what more to do.
It was not meant for her to see this doom—
Perhaps the Reaper would collect his due. . . .

TRIBUTES

A PAGE FROM JACK'S DIARY

Adam Bolivar

I sing the Lady Ashiel,
    Whose witchcraft none could quell,
Who in the gloom of Night would dwell
    To conjure fiends from Hell.

I wandered far across the land,
    And always heard the same:
From ice of north to southern sand
    Is feared this Lady's name.

And so into the waste I struck
    To find the Sorceress,
And though I knew I pushed my luck,
    I frankly must confess

That more than e'en her dæmon ways,
    Her pulchritude was told,
And for a sight I trudged for days
    That fairness to behold.

At last I came where once she dwelt,
    A ruin, black and cold,
And there before a grave I knelt:
    Rain-worn and very old.

Embracing it with prickly thorn,
    A crimson rose there grew;
The Lady's lover bode forlorn—
    I wept for love so true.

My Lady of the Nightshade Flower

K. A. Opperman

For Ashley Dioses
In Tribute

My lady of the nightshade flower,
Your eyes of twilit dwale
Have gazed upon Endymion,
Who dreams in yonder vale.

My lady of the nightshade flower,
Your poison purple lips
Have whispered spells in blooming hells
Where honeyed nectar drips.

My lady of the nightshade flower,
Your sable, fragrant hair
Is crowned with wreaths whose blossom breathes
Dim drugs upon the air.

My lady of the nightshade flower,
Whose flesh is petal-pale,
O sing your songs, for evening longs
For belladonna's bale.

Upon Reading *Diary of a Sorceress*

Michael Fantina

Both in and out of darkling dreams I've read
Her splendid poems that most bewitching are.
Supple Siren she, consort to some Czar
Or some great Pharaoh vanished, long since dead.
With magics from her poetry it's said
She moves through Space and Time, an avatar
Of realms that circle some stupendous star;
Her suitors tethered to a magic thread.

Her words like spells that lullingly enchant,
Seduce the mind and heart to worlds outré,
To Siren-haunted coasts lapped by a sea
Whose tides send up one long eternal chant
About that most beguiling, dream-wrought bay.
Both sorceress and poet, this is she.

ASHIEL'S GARDEN

D. L. Myers

In Ashiel's garden of gloom,
There is no dappled sunlight at midday,
And the silence is only cut
By the grim scratching of twisted, barbed vines
That sway and shudder in the wind.

Her lithe form swathed in tattered silk,
She plays the air with graceful sweeps and arcs—
Her hands painting the wind with vile
Images of things foul, fey and soulless
That the black garden feeds upon.

Her hands still at last, she grasps
The thin, dire skull that lies between her breasts
And surveys the grey, leprous grounds—
The black twined things that strain in the now slack air
Reaching for her like lost lovers.

The light slowly fades to twilight
And cold stars begin to burn above her.
As the garden sinks into night,
Her eyes flare with starlight
Until her form is lost and all that remains are the stars.

AFTERWORD

I began to have a taste for writing at a young age. I believe I wrote my first short story, about an alien and a boy playing with marbles in a treehouse, in first grade. My dad was a writer and encouraged my creativity, and though we both loved fantasy, he wrote mostly for children. When my older brother started kindergarten, my dad became very involved with our schools and wrote children's poetry for the school newsletter. When I started school, he read to my class, both poetry and short stories.

But as I grew older, my tastes for different genres changed. I loved reading horror, so when I discovered Edgar Allan Poe in seventh grade by reading "The Black Cat," my obsession for writing horror began. After reading that story, I wrote my first horror tale, which involved some neighborhood children entering a haunted house and never returning.

Then one piece of work changed my entire tune: "Annabel Lee." A poem that was dark, fascinating, and amazing. An amazing poem—who had ever heard of such a thing? Well, at age twelve that was what we all thought, I'm sure. It was nothing like the children's poetry my dad wrote and read to me. Already an avid reader of fantasy and horror, I decided to combine both genres into what I knew about poetry and then wrote it every day. I wanted more than anything to have a collection of poetry published as my first of, hopefully, many published works.

I stopped writing poetry after high school and during college to focus on other writing projects. When I met Kyle Opperman, in my early twenties, he showed me the wonderful world of weird poetry and fiction. After reading poetry by Clark Ashton Smith, H. P. Lovecraft, George Sterling, and David Park Barnitz, I was determined to write and make a serious collection of dark, weird, and fantastical poetry.

Diary of a Sorceress emerged from a poem that Kyle and I collaborated on, shortly after we got together. The poem, "Sorcerously Entwined," is about a Sorcerer's unrequited love for a sorceress. The Sorcerer planned to kill himself with a brew he created using plants from her garden, but found out that by drinking it he would be connected to her. Their fates would be entwined and if he died, she would as well. Together, they try to find a way to fix this, yet the Sorceress ends up dying in their attempt. The Sorcerer must make a deal with a demon to enter the Otherworld to find her soul. Time is racing as a powerful demoness, out of jealousy, tries to stop them from reuniting. Their lives as Sorceress and Sorcerer come to a tragic end, yet their story continues in another life.

Diary of a Sorceress is based after the Sorceress in the poem. This is her diary. The book starts with a prelude describing a few themes to expect and then is followed by four sections or diary entries. The first Sorceress-themed poem is titled after the book and sets the story. It describes how she first came to know about the Sorcerer and shows a scathing letter she wrote in response to a love letter the Sorcerer sent her.

The diary is structured from light to dark, hopefully to give the feeling of descending into the darker parts of the Sorceress's world. The first entry, "Atop the Crystal Moon," contains poems of a fantastical nature, both dark and light-hearted. The second entry, "Kiss the Stars," contains fantastical nature-based themes. The third entry, "Star Lighting," starts off with darkly romantic poetry and leads into the more erotic sort. The fourth and last entry, "On a Dreamland's Moon," is the biggest section and contains horror. The last poem of the book concludes with a Sorceress poem that ends her story and hints at a new life and start of a new diary.

—ASHLEY DIOSES

ACKNOWLEDGMENTS

"The Abandoned Garden," first published in *Halloween Howlings* (Fall 2015).

"Bathory in Red," first published in *Weirdbook* No. 33 (Fall 2016).

"Blood Siren's Alcove," first published in *Weirdbook* No. 33 (Fall 2016).

"Can I Stop Your Heart?" first published in *Dark River Press* (Winter 2012).

"Carathis," first published in *Spectral Realms* No. 1 (Summer 2014).

"Castle Csejthe," first published in *Weirdbook* No. 31 (September 14, 2015).

"Celestial Mysteries," first published in *Beyond the Cosmic Veil, Into the Chaos* (Horrified Press, 2015).

"Daemonolatry," *Walk On The Weird Side* edited by Joseph S. Pulver, Sr. (August 2017).

"Dark Poet of My Heart," first published in *Spectral Realms* No. 5 (Summer 2016).

"Dark Valentine," first published in *The Literary Hatchet* No. 15 (August 22, 2016).

"Dark Valentine II," *The Literary Hatchet* No. 16 (December 14, 2016).

"Diary of a Sorceress," first published in *Skelos* No. 1 (May 26, 2016).

"The Easter Lily," first published in *Cyäegha* No. 16 (Summer 2016).

"Even Madness Cannot Hide," first published in *Spectral Realms* No. 3 (Summer 2015).

"Ever Fair," first published in *Spectral Realms* No. 5 (Summer 2016).

"Fallen Atlantis," first published in *Spectral Realms* No. 5 (Summer 2016).

"Fire Sprite," first published in *Feverish Fiction* No. 6 (Spring 2017).

"The Fires of Summer," first published in *The Literary Hatchet* No. 18 (August 2017).

"Ghoul Mistress," first published in *HWA Poetry Showcase* (August 7, 2016).

"A Glamorous Touch," first published in *Dark River Press* (Winter 2012).

"The Glass Vial," first published in *The Audient Void* No. 1 (June 19, 2016).

"Goetia," first published in *Mythopoesis* No. 19 (Winter 2016).

"Graveyard Blossom," first published in *Halloween Howlings* (Fall 2015).

"The Hands of Chaos," *Test Patterns* (Planet X Publications 2017).

"Horror," first published in *Spectral Realms* No. 1 (Summer 2014).

"Illva," first published in *Spectral Realms* No. 4 (Winter 2016).

"Kiss the Stars," first published in *Spectral Realms* No. 1 (Summer 2014).

"Labyrinthine King," first published in *47-16: Short Fiction & Poetry Inspired by David Bowie, Volume 1,* ed. Chris Thompson (Penny Dreadful Publications, 2016).

"Lady Death," *Obscurum: The Death Issue* No. 2 (Summer 2017).

"Ligeia," first published in *Spectral Realms* No. 2 (Winter 2015).

"Lord of the Deep," *The Stylus* (Summer 2017).

"Lover's Witch," first published in *Weird Fiction Review* No. 5 (Fall 2015).

"Maenads," first published in *Necronomicum: The Magazine of Weird Erotica* No. 4 (October 17, 2015).

"The Medallion," first published in *Beyond the Cosmic Veil, Into the Chaos* (Horrified Press, 2015).

"Medusa's Mirror," first published in *Xnoybis* No. 2 (December 22, 2015).

"Mircalla," first published in *Gothic Blue Book* No. 5 (October 28, 2015).

"Morning's Moon," first published in *The Literary Hatchet* No. 13 (December 25, 2015).

"My Corpse, My Groom," first published in *The Audient Void* No. 1 (June 19, 2016).

"I. Nadia," *Devolution Z January 2017: The Horror Magazine* Vol. 16 (January 2, 2017).

"The Necro-Conjuring Sorceress," first published in *Weirdbook* No. 32 (June 16, 2016).

"Night Play," first published in *Spectral Realms* No. 6 (Winter 2016).

"Nitokris," first published in *Weird Fiction Review* No. 7 (Fall 2016).

"Nyarlathotep," first published in 2012 Nyarlathotep Tuscano Wine Label (2016).

"On a Dreamland's Moon," first published in *Black Wings VI: New Tales of Lovecraftian Horror*, ed. S. T. Joshi (PS Publishing, 2017).

"Painted in Blood," first published in *Inanna Rising: Women Forged in Fire*, ed. Amanda M. Lyons (CreateSpace, 2015).

"Panic," *Xnoybis No. 3: In Praise of Pan* (Spring 2017).

"The Perfect Rose," first published in *Spectral Realms* No. 3 (Summer 2015).

"Prelude—My Dark Diary," first published in *Gothic Blue Book* No. 5 (October 28, 2015).

"A Queen in Hell," first published in *Spectral Realms* No. 3 (Summer 2015).

"The Rotting Goddess," first published in *The Audient Void* No. 2 (Fall 2016).

"Scarlet Autumn Aurora," first published in *Ravenwood Quarterly* No. 2 (Fall 2016).

"A Sea of Snow and Frost," *Walk On The Weird Side* edited Joseph S. Pulver, Sr. (August 2017).

"Selkie," *The Stylus* (Summer 2017).

"Sephora," *Weirdbook* No. 34 (Winter 2017).

"Siren's Song," first published in *Spectral Realms* No. 6 (Winter 2016).

"A Sorcerous Tome," first published in *The Crimson Tome* by K. A. Opperman (Hippocampus Press, 2015).

"Sweet Renegade," first published in *Dark River Press* (Winter 2012).

"They Sing in Whispers," first published in *Ravenwood Quarterly* No. 3 (Fall 2017).

"A Sorceress's Final Vision," *The Audient Void: A Journal of Weird Fiction and Dark Fantasy* No. 3 (April 13, 2017).

"Twisted Trails of Thought," first published in *The Crimson Tome* by K. A. Opperman (Hippocampus Press, 2015).

"Under the Chrysanthemums," first published in *Blood Moon Rising* No. 51 (Winter 2012).

"A Valkyrie's Vendetta," first published in *Barbarian Crowns* (Barbwire Butterfly Books, 2015).

"Venus," first published in *Eternal Haunted Summer* (Winter 2016).

"Vexteria," first published in *Spectral Realms* No. 2 (Winter 2015).

"Winter Witch," first published in *Winter Horror Days,* ed. David Lucarelli (Omnium Gatherum Media, 2015).

"Witch Lord of the Hunt," first published in *Eternal Haunted Summer* (Spring 2016).

"Witch's Love," first published in *Spectral Realms* No. 2 (Winter 2015).

"With a Love So Vile," first published in *Spectral Realms* No. 4 (Winter 2016).